ROBERT LIVINGSTON AL

SHARON'S ARIA

from ELMER GANTRY

For Voice and Piano

Libretto by

HERSCHEL GARFEIN

based on the novel by Sinclair Lewis

duration: circa 3 minutes and 45 seconds

C.F. PETERS CORPORATION

A member of the EDITION PETERS GROUP

FRANKFURT/M. · LEIPZIG · LONDON · NEW YORK

Special thanks to the following people, without whose help, hard work and support ELMER GANTRY could never have been created, performed or published:

Paula Stark, Vicki Bernstein, Blan and Kay Aldridge, Lorraine Hunt Lieberson, Charles Schwager, Robert S. Lee, Sally Lee, William Shuyler, Neil Rosini; John Hoomes, Carol Penterman and Nashville Opera Association; Rev. Arthur Woody, Rev. Darryl MacLaren; Jedediah Wheeler, Susan Cole, John and Rose Cali, Geoffrey Newman, Richard Lynde, Mark Heimerdinger and Montclair State University; Boris Kucharsky, Fred Hersch, Richard Dyer, Yuval Sharon, Greg Emetaz; Heather J. Buchanan, Jeffrey Gall, Paul Hostetter, William Boggs; Evva Pryor, Eugene Winick and MacIntosh and Otis; Roger McClean, Gene Caprioglio, Héctor Colón and C.F. Peters Corporation.

for Micaela, Hadi and Lev

Robert Aldridge and Herschel Garfein

*Premiere Production by Nashville Opera Association,
Nashville, Tennessee, November 16, 2007;
Montclair State University, Montclair, New Jersey,
January 23, 2008.*

Cast

Elmer Gantry	Keith Phares
Sharon Falconer	Jennifer Rivera
Frank Shallard	Vale Rideout /
	William Ferguson
Eddie Fislinger	Frank Kelley
Lulu Baines	Malinda Haslett
Reverend Baines	Brian Banion
T.J. Rigg	Kristopher Irmiter /
	David Salsbery Fry
Mrs. Baines	Olivia Ward /
	Janara Kellerman
Revival Singer	Chauncey Packer
Stage Director:	John Hoomes
Conductor:	William Boggs /
	Paul Hostetter
Set Designer:	Takeshi Kata
Lighting Designer:	Robert Wierzel
Costume Designer:	Camille Assaf
Opera Workshop/Chorus Master:	Jeffrey Gall/
	Heather J. Buchanan,
	Amy Tate-Williams

SHARON'S ARIA
from Elmer Gantry *Act I, scene iv*

Sister Sharon Falconer is an evangelist, the head of a modest ministry traveling the Mid-western United States in the first decade of the 20th century. Her spiritual gifts and her honest connection to the divine have brought her some renown and a devoted local following.

Sharon's Aria takes place at one of her tent revivals on a summer night in 1907. A crowd of curious onlookers (including Elmer Gantry) has gathered outside the tent to try to catch a glimpse of Sharon. She steps out of the tent opening to encourage them to join her ("Oh, it's joy, isn't it?"). After a moment, her thoughts turn inward, and she slips into a simple, profoundly personal reverie ("The sun embraces the stony earth"). Her coda ("No wonder the angels sing to each other") is a brief, unprepared epiphany that vanishes as quickly as it appeared.

Sharon: *(beginning o.s., growing louder as she approaches the tent opening:)*

> Oh...It's joy, isn't it? A joy so pure... A joy so pure... Can you feel it?
> Friends outside the tent... Can you feel a little of that joy now?
> That's the Lord... That's the Lord...

(She is now visible at the tent opening. Her right hand is raised, palm forward, her hair is streaming and her face is flushed, perspiring. She wears a straight white robe tied with a ruby-colored cinch; its wide, slashed sleeves fall away from her bare arms. The congregants sense that she is about to address them. They stop the hymn)

> The sun embraces the stony earth,
> Sweet rain caresses the land,
> And pure is the joy that cradles the heart
> Touched by Thee, touched by Thee.
> No wonder the angels sing to each other.

(Some congregants are kneeling, heads bowed. Sharon slowly advances down this line of penitents, bestowing a silent or a whispered blessing.)

Sharon's Aria

from Elmer Gantry
An Opera in Two Acts

Libretto by Herschel Garfein

Music by Robert Livingston Aldridge

She closes her eyes in private prayer.

And pure_____ is the

joy that cra - dles the_____ heart_____

Touched by_____

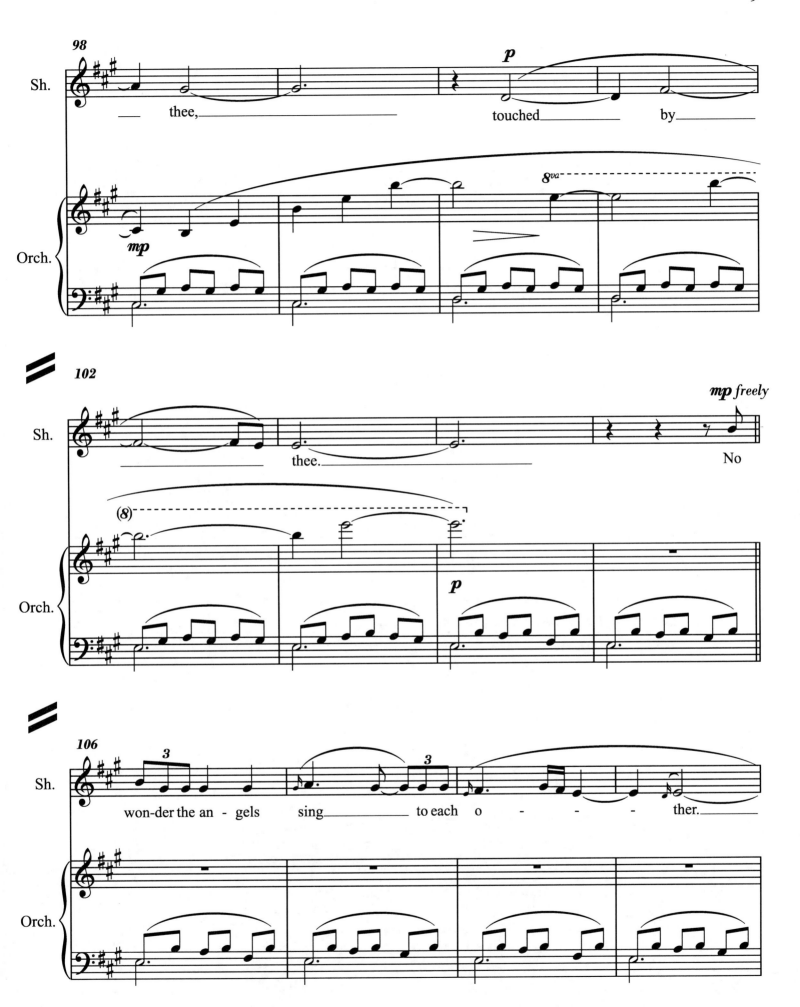

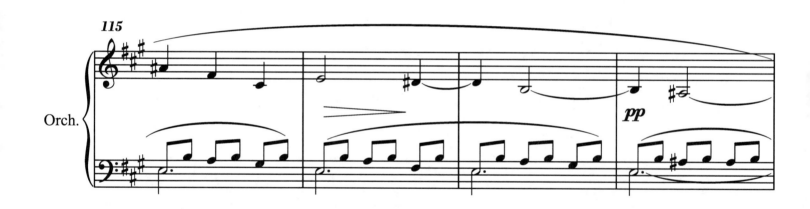

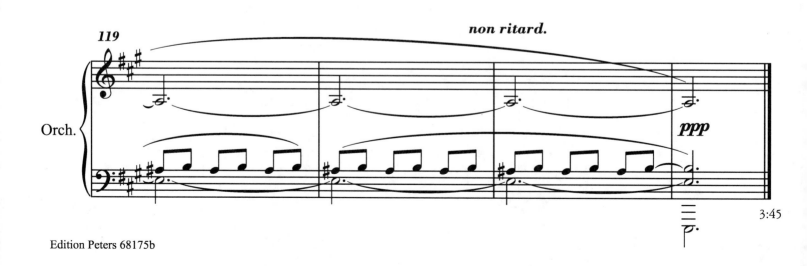

3:45